JEREMIAH, MEET THE 20TH CENTURY

James W. Sire

---

12 Studies
in Jeremiah

InterVarsity Press
Downers Grove
Illinois 60515

Second printing, February 1976

*InterVarsity Press is the book
publishing division of Inter-Varsity
Christian Fellowship, a student
movement active on campus at
hundreds of universities, colleges
and schools of nursing. For
information about local and
regional activities, write IVCF,
233 Langdon, Madison, WI 53703.*

*ISBN 0-87784-641-3
Library of Congress Catalog
Card Number: 74-31846*

*Printed in the United
States of America*

CONTENTS

Introduction

Christians today are barraged by a host of voices. Some say, "Look, you Christians have had your way in the West for two thousand years. You've botched it. It's time to look elsewhere. Maybe an Eastern guru or two would do us a world of good." Others are subtly soothing: "Come on to Washington [or, up here to the state capitol]. Put your weight behind my campaign. It'll do you and your Christian cause a lot of good." Others say, "Give up. Put away your antique belief in God. If he existed and were really in control of the world, then we wouldn't be in such a mess." And others yet say, "We're a Christian country, God's country. Don't worry about the world's crises. God will take care of America." Even some who call themselves Christian say, "Every man has a right to his own religion, you know. Let's lay aside our distinctive theologies and be tolerant."

Voices calling for allegiance, programs proposed by a dozen and one public and private agencies: Stop the bombing! Impeach the President! America: Love It or Leave It! Honk if you love Jesus!

What's a sincere Christian to do? Does the Bible give any light? Isn't our modern situation unique, unparalleled? The answer is a resounding *no*. There was once before such a situation as ours—a decaying culture, a nation in decline, beset by political and religious ferment within and without. And there was a prophet of God to that nation, a man through whom God spoke hard words of judgment, wise words of counsel, great words of hope. His name—Jeremiah. The country—Judah.

Consider the political times. Judah is precariously placed between two huge foreign powers—Babylon to the north, Egypt to the south. The Babylonians are besieging its capital city of Jerusalem, while the Egyptians are apparently coming to Judah's aid. The king calls in the most famous prophet of the day—a man who has been warning that Jerusalem will fall to the Babylonians and has been imprisoned for demoralizing the soldiers. The king is anxious to see this prophet change his mind, for so far his words have been altogether too well confirmed by events. What will the prophet do? Hold to his prophecy and return to captivity in a muddy cistern or change his mind and be released?

Consider the religious times. The worship of Jehovah, the one true God, has been abandoned or adulterated by worship of Canaanite and Assyrian deities. The priests are so apostate that the voice of God is no longer heard in the land, and the average man in Judah is largely unaware of God's laws. Then, in steps a prophet, the son of a priestly family in a small town near Jerusalem. He delivers a biting indictment of Judah's spiritual condition, associating *lack* of true spirituality with the kind of worship going on at the temple. Moreover, he does this in the courtyard of the temple itself. When he stirs up the animosity of the religious leaders and is arrested, what happens? Can truth defend the teller of it?

Consider the Jewish people. They are faced with a single prophet who counsels capitulation to a foreign power and a group of prophets who counsel continued war. Who is the true prophet? Who shall the king, the princes and the people believe?

The Man and His Time

The days of Jeremiah's long life, at least sixty years, were fraught with tension—political, religious, personal. In one of the richest of biblical "biographies," the book of Jeremiah opens up the life and times of a great prophet and a great man. It reveals a person with fierce integrity, great sensitivity to human need, deep devotion to the God of Abraham, Isaac and Jacob, an abiding loyalty to God's Word, and a warm compassion for the people of God.

He was a lonely man who faced discouragement when God seemed so far from realizing his purposes for Judah. Still, he had a few faithful friends, not the least of whom was his secretary Baruch. Called "the weeping prophet," he left many hints of hope for the future and wrote (or dictated) what came to be called The Book of Consolation.

Jeremiah's appearance in Judah was a watershed of Jewish religious consciousness. God called him to be a prophet in 626 B.C.: "Behold, I have put my words in your mouth. See, I have set you this day over nations and over kingdoms, to pluck up and to break down, to destroy and to overthrow, to build and to plant" (Jer. 1:9-10). At this time Judah, the so-called Southern Kingdom with its capital in Jerusalem, was beginning to break free from vassalage to Assyria and to establish an independence not known since Ahaz had subjected them to Assyrian control in about 730 B.C. During the early years of Jeremiah's ministry, King Josiah conducted a religious reform based on a copy of the law newly discovered in the temple. But apostasy deriving from too close an association with Assyria and the local Canaanite customs was still rife.

By the time Jeremiah died, at least forty years after his call, Judah had lost its great King Josiah in a foolish battle (against Egypt at Megiddo in 609 B.C.), it had suffered under a series of bad kings and a new vassalage, this time to

Babylon, and in trying to throw off this yoke it had found itself totally wiped out. The fall of Jerusalem in 587 B.C. marked the eradication of the Jewish nation. Its best men—leaders, artisans, craftsmen—were either killed or exiled to Babylon where they stayed until Ezra and Nehemiah returned to rebuild the city and the temple decades later.

It was a time of much religious activity, with Ezekiel in Babylon (from 597 B.C.) and others such as Nahum, Zephaniah and Habakkuk holding forth the Word of God. The most important single prophecy belongs, however, to Jeremiah who announces the days to come when God "will make a new covenant with the house of Israel and the house of Judah" (Jer. 31:31), a prophecy which began to be fulfilled when Jesus was crucified and resurrected and when the Holy Spirit was given at Pentecost.

But there is no need to comment further. Jeremiah himself tells the story in masterful words of poetry and prose. For a brief overview of the historical events in Jeremiah's lifetime see pages 114-16.

Purpose of the Studies

The present guide is designed to help readers of the prophet get over certain hurdles posed by occasional obscurities and the (at first) confusing organization of the book of Jeremiah. For an unraveling of the overall structure of the book, see the outline on pages 113-14.

Each study takes up a different aspect of Jeremiah's message or a different event in Jeremiah's life. The sequence is generally historical and spans the forty years from Jeremiah's call to after the fall of Jerusalem. Since twelve studies cannot exhaust the material in Jeremiah's fifty-two chapters, each study has a topical focus—for example, the character of the Word of God, the nature of true and false prophets, the importance of true worship of the one true God, and the requisites for God's guidance in one's life. Through this topical approach, each study suggests implications for life in our own era.

In a real sense Jeremiah's circumstances were much like ours. He faced a time of severe religious apostasy in the very center of orthodox worship. He found himself unable to support the political stance of national leaders who had become corrupt, building for themselves sumptuous living quarters at great expense. He watched as his country relied on a foreign power that always before had proven a false friend. He saw his nation go from independence to vassalage to total destruction. He watched as the chosen people of God refused to acknowledge God or to repent and return to fidelity—even as the results of their apostasy were being worked out in the capture of Judah and the destruction of Jerusalem.

How far does this parallel our time? As I write this in the wake of the Watergate situation and the resignation of first a Vice-President and then a President, it appears that the problems in the U.S. are more internal than external. We see the parallels of moral decay, political corruption and spiritual rot. But will we see our own nation go through a similar destruction? A study of Jeremiah can, I believe, give us some perspective. Certainly it will suggest to us as Christians a number of specific options for action now—before destruction, if it comes, is fully upon us.

How to Use This Study

Besides a copy of this book, only two other items are required—a modern translation of the Bible and a notebook. The Revised Standard Version was used in the preparation of the guide, so it is the version most easily used, but the New English Bible and the New American Standard Version are also highly recommended. Paraphrases such as the Living Bible are helpful for comparison and readability but should not form the basis of serious study.

A notebook will be necessary if you wish to retain much of what you learn. Writing aids memory! And notes help you organize and clarify your own thoughts.

Each person participating in a group discussion based on

this guide is expected to prepare before coming to the discussion. (Of course, the guide can be used by individuals for independent study as well.) Groups should set aside at least an hour for discussion. Every one of these studies could easily extend to 90 minutes, so group leaders will need to use discretion so that time is used to best advantage (help is found on pp. 89-112). Here are some suggestions for group members as they study individually.

After you pray for the Holy Spirit's guidance, the *first* step is to *read* and *reread* the focal passage listed at the head of the study.

Second, try to answer each question listed, jotting your conclusions in your notebook. Make a note of difficulties you encounter and bring them up when your discussion group meets.

Third, seriously reflect on the implications for your own life. Make a list of all the actions you believe you should now take based on your insights from the Scripture.

Fourth, pray for wisdom as you prepare to share your insights with members of your group and with your friends. And pray for others in the group as they are studying this passage and applying it in their life.

At the end of each study you will find a suggestion for additional reading; this is designed to carry you further into the focal topic. The following materials are more general and are listed in their order of importance as further guides to understanding the book of Jeremiah: R. K. Harrison, *Jeremiah and Lamentations* (IVP); *The New Bible Dictionary* (Eerdmans); *The New Bible Commentary: Revised* (Eerdmans and IVP).

Notes for the leader are found on pages 89-112. These are designed to help leaders prepare the study and lead the discussion. Although certain knotty issues are elucidated, group members should refrain from relying on these notes rather than doing hard and creative thinking for themselves. If you are studying this material on your own, however, you may wish to consult these notes as a final measure.

THE PROPHET'S CALL 1

text:
Jeremiah 1:1-19
purposes:
1/*To be introduced to Jeremiah the man*
2/*To consider Jeremiah's call as an example of one way God sets an individual apart for a special purpose*
3/*To reflect on the ways God may be speaking to us as individuals*

Jeremiah's call to be a prophet was dramatic and convincing. Later it became for him a rock of certainty when he faced the tough problems of a public ministry. To grasp the implications of God's call to Jeremiah can set our lives in perspective even in the twentieth century.

1. How do verses 1-3 date Jeremiah's ministry? (See Appendix C, p. 116. Note: Two kings are missing from Jeremiah's list—Jehoahaz and Jehoiachin—probably because their reigns were each only three months long.)

____

____

2. How long, therefore, did Jeremiah prophesy? (The thirteenth year of Josiah's reign is 627 B.C.; the fall of Jerusalem is 587; but Jeremiah's life and work extend even beyond this. See Jer. 40—44.)

____

3. How did God let Jeremiah know he was to be a prophet (v. 4)? Of what significance is it that God "spoke" to Jeremiah? What advantages do words have over such possible means as "strong urge" or "feeling" or "omen" or "desire to be God's spokesman"?

____

____

____

____

____

4. When did God know he was going to call Jeremiah (v.5)? In what way does verse 5 parallel Psalm 139:15 and Isaiah 49:1, 5? What data is unique to Jeremiah 1:5? What does this suggest about God's character as a planner and his recognition of the uniqueness of each individual?

____

____

____

____

____

5. Is Jeremiah's response to God's call (v. 6) reasonable? What does God think of Jeremiah's response? Why does he think this (vv. 7-8)?

____

 ____

6. In addition to addressing him in words, how does God convey his message to Jeremiah (v. 9)? What is the meaning of this action? How do you know?

7. What is to be Jeremiah's general function (v. 10)? What kinds of words is he to speak? To whom (vv. 5, 10)?

8. In verses 11-19 Jeremiah is given two visions, both of which the Lord explains in words. What is the first vision and its meaning? (Note: The Hebrew word for *almond* is formed from the root of the verb "to be wakeful" or "to watch." The almond blossoms early in spring.) Of what value can this vision be to Jeremiah as he performs his job as prophet?

9. What is the second vision and its meaning (vv. 13-19)? What will Jeremiah have to do in the face of the present false religion within Judah and the coming invasion?

10. Who will be Jeremiah's enemies (v. 18)? Why should Jeremiah be confident in the face of coming disaster? What will happen if Jeremiah cowers (v. 17)?

11. To summarize, consider Jeremiah's call, these visions and the Lord's words in verse 19. What help do you think they gave him as a man about to begin a prophetic role?

12. What can you point to in your own life that sets it in perspective as Jeremiah's life is set in perspective here? Are these things you are pointing to "visions" or "experiences" without verbal content, or is some aspect of God's spoken word involved? What aspect?

13. Only a few are called to be prophets like Jeremiah, but all of us are given the opportunity to respond to God's special call to us as individuals. Can you point to a time when you first heard God's call? How did you respond?

14. Is he calling you again now? What, for example, in this first chapter of Jeremiah is challenging to you? How are you responding? Take time out *now* to speak to God about it, and come to the group discussion with something to share in regard to your own developing walk with God.

additional reading

Paul Little, Affirming the Will of God *(IVP)*
Francis A. Schaeffer, He Is There and He Is Not Silent *(Tyndale House Publishers)*

THE HISTORICAL BACKGROUND 2

texts:
2 Kings 20:1–25:30; focal passage 2 Kings 20:12–23:37 (parallel in 2 Chron. 29:1–36:23)
purposes:
1/*To understand the basic historical and cultural background of Jeremiah's life and times*
2/*To grasp the framework in which God acts in reference to the Jewish nation*
3/*To become aware of the consequences of false religion and social injustice*

This study will probably take you longer to prepare than others in this book. It focuses on the historical events preceding and surrounding the life of Jeremiah and raises few questions of modern application. Many which could be raised are treated in later studies. In some ways, however, nothing is more practical than a solid grasp of the past, especially in understanding God's word to men over there and back then. Often this is a prerequisite for hearing God's word to us here and now.

1. In a column, list the kings in the order in which they reigned over Judah (the Southern Kingdom, headquarters Jerusalem) from Hezekiah to Zedekiah. In parallel columns indicate (1) whether their reign was good or evil in the sight of God, (2) which of the three great empirical powers

(Assyria, Chaldea [Babylon] or Egypt) they favored, (3) which they served as vassals and (4) which they considered enemies. (See the Brief Chronology of Judah, pp. 114-16, and the list of the kings of Judah, p. 116.)

____

____

____

____

____

____

____

____

2. The writers of Kings and Chronicles make general judgments concerning the basic rightness or wrongness of each king. Do they mention gray areas in good kings or good aspects of bad kings? (See, for example, 2 Chron. 33: 10-20.) Explain. Illustrate.

____

____

____

____

3. Under whose reign was the exile to Babylon first prophesied (2 Kings 20:12-19; see also Mic. 3:12 and 4:10 which date to the same general time and Jer. 26:18)? Who made the prophecy? Under what circumstances? Was it linked at this point with "judgment" for evil? What does this suggest about the complexity of the historical factors which lead to major events in national history?

4. How did the king take the news that his sons would be taken away to Babylon? At this stage of the king's life what seems to characterize him?

5. What kind of king was Hezekiah's son? What does this suggest about Hezekiah himself (2 Kings 21:1-19)?

6. On what aspect of Manasseh's reign does the chronicler focus? Suggest why. What does this activity lead to? What else characterized Manasseh's reign (21:16)?

7. List the various apostate religious practices mentioned

in 21:1-9. Why is this so abominable to the Lord (vv. 7-8;

see also 1 Kings 9:1-9)? Does Judah have any "excuse" for its apostasy? Could they have been unaware of the seriousness of their action (Ex. 34:13 and Deut. 12:3)? (Note: The Ashera was an image of a Canaanite goddess associated with Baal.)

8. What specifically is prophesied in 21:10-15? How long does it take for this prophecy to be fulfilled? (Note: Manasseh's reign was 686-42 B.C. The fall of Jerusalem took place in 587.)

9. What changes, if any, did the reign of Amon bring? How was his reign brought to an end (21:19-26)?

10. How did Josiah become king (21:24)? At what age (22:1)? How long did he serve (21:2)?

11. What happened in the eighteenth year of his reign? (Note: Because of 2 Chron. 34:3 and for other reasons, the exact date is in question. The dates 631-628 are often suggested.) How was the book of the law (probably Deuteronomy or a part of it) found? What does this tell us about the time when Josiah began his religious reform? What was Josiah's reaction when it was read to him? Why?

____

____

____

____

12. Whose counsel did Josiah seek? List all those he consulted.

____

____

____

13. What did the prophetess Huldah say? Why?

____

____

____

14. How did the king then respond? What does this whole section on Josiah (2 Kings 22:1—23:30) suggest about the importance of knowing God's Word?

____

____

____

15. What reforms did Josiah institute (23:4-15, 19-25)? (Note: These were a response to a *hearing* of the Word; a comparison with John 13:17 is instructive.)

16. What worship did Josiah restore (23:21-23)?

17. Did the restoration and reforms of Josiah prevent the fulfillment of the earlier predictive prophecy concerning Jerusalem and Judah (23:26-27)? Why?

18. How did Josiah's reign end (23:29-31)? (Note: Pharaoh Neco was coming to the aid of Assyria in its fight against the Babylonians. Josiah foolishly engaged him in battle and lost [609 B.C.].)

19. Under whose vassalage did Jehoahaz serve and what happened to him (23:31-34)?

20. How did Jehoiakim come to be king (23:34-35)? How long did he reign (23:36-37)?

____

____

21. How can we keep from making Judah's error of "losing" the Word? Is there a sense in which we ourselves and our own religious institutions have lost it already?

____

____

____

____

This brings us roughly to the year 609 B.C. when Jehoiakim's reign began. Jeremiah was called to be a prophet in 627 B.C.; chapters 1—6 of the book of Jeremiah contain prophecies uttered during Josiah's reign up to 609 B.C. Study 3 takes up one of the more memorable of Jeremiah's sermons. It was delivered at the beginning of Jehoiakim's reign, the point at which the present study ends. Later historical developments from 609 to 587 B.C. (described in 2 Kings 24—25) will be taken up in the context of Jeremiah's prophecy.

additional reading

Samuel J. Schultz, The Old Testament Speaks *(Harper), pp. 209-28*

Robert Munger, My Heart—Christ's Home *(IVP)*

THE GREAT TEMPLE SERMON 3

texts:
Jeremiah 26:1-24; 7:1–10:25
purposes:
1/*To see Jeremiah in action and under tension*
2/*To see how God viewed the religious and moral life of Jeremiah's time*
3/*To consider how he must then view our lives and our society*
4/*To begin to take action on the basis of God's desire to see righteousness prevail*

The Temple Sermon given at the beginning of Jehoiakim's reign (c. 608 B.C.) is one of the most famous sermons of all time. It was delivered "when pagan Canaanite rituals were appearing again in the cultic rites of Judah" (Harrison, p. 85). We will consider first the historical setting and the immediate results to Jeremiah (26:1-24), and then the sermon itself, a relatively long passage (7:1—10:25) which we will treat by focusing on representative sections. Before answering the following questions, read both passages carefully.

1. From whom does the sermon derive (26:1-2)?

---

2. Where is Jeremiah to deliver the sermon (26:2)? To

whom? What is its purpose (26:3)?

3. How do verses 4-6 summarize the Temple Sermon? What are its main parts?

4. Do the people respond as the Lord wishes (26:7-9)? What disturbs them?

5. What happens to Jeremiah as a result of the sermon? Summarize 26:10-19 to clarify *who* did what to *whom*. (Note: The "princes" of verse 10 are officials of the palace and not "royalty" as such; in verses 7-8, 11 the Septuagint adds the word *false* to the word *prophets* as is clearly implied by the context.)

6. What is Jeremiah's own argument in self-defense (26: 12-15)? Why does Jeremiah consider himself innocent (v. 15)? Could Jeremiah be considered a modern revolutionary? Why? (Compare Acts 4:19-20. How do Peter and John before the Sanhedrin advance a parallel argument for their action?)

7. How do allegiances change as the trial proceeds? Why? What precedent for not convicting Jeremiah do the elders find (26:18-19)? (Recall the prophecy of Mic. 3:12 and 4:10, as we considered it in study 2.)

8. Consider the case of Uriah, another true prophet of the Lord: How was his treatment different from Jeremiah's (26:20-24)? (Note: Some have suggested that Uriah was considered a traitor because he fled to Egypt and had to be extradited—Harrison, p. 128.) What does verse 24 suggest about why Jeremiah's life was spared at this point?

9. Explain the significance of the phrase three times repeated in 7:4. (See 7:10-15.)

10. What does the Lord require of Judah (7:5-6)?

11. Consider in more detail three charges God makes against Judah. First, the charge of idolatry or false religion: From 7:16-18, 30-31, describe the religious practices of Judah.

12. From 10:3-15, compare the attributes of the false gods or idols with those of the Lord. Why is Judah's idolatry so foolish? What conclusion should Judah reach?

13. List the consequences of worshiping false gods (7:20, 32-34; 8:1-3; 10:11, 14; compare Rom. 6:23).

14. Consider a second charge—deceit. How does 9:1-6 describe the people of Judah? What will be the consequences (9:7-11)?

15. In the light of the Lord's desire to forgive the repentant (7:5-7), consider a third charge—stubborn unrepentance. How does 8:4-13 describe the people of Judah? What would the Lord like to do (8:13)? What is his attitude to Judah in 8:18-22? What is the missing ingredient for the Lord's healing of the land?

16. Which, if any, of the Lord's indictments in the Temple Sermon would be true in your country, your city, your church, your own life? What do you think God is calling you to do about it? Be prepared to discuss this question as your group meets.

additional reading

Francis A. Schaeffer, The Church before the Watching World *(IVP)*

ADULTERY AND APOSTASY 4

texts:
Jeremiah 2–3 and selected biblical passages
purposes:
1/*To grasp the significance of fidelity in faith and in marriage*
2/*To consider our response as Christians in a society where adultery is commonplace and in a religious environment where apostasy is hardly recognized*

The major fault Jeremiah finds with Judah is apostasy or false religion. Over and over he uses the imagery of sexual infidelity to picture this state of affairs. Why should this language be appropriate? Are the two themes connected in more than literary ways? The answers to these questions take us beyond Jeremiah's prophecy, but Jeremiah provides a good focal point for the broader subject.

1. How are the twin themes of adultery and apostasy linked together in the following passages? In which sin does Jeremiah seem more interested? (Answer this for each separate passage.)

2:1-2 ____________________

2:20, 23-25, 33 (cf. 17:2) ____________________

3:1-3 ____________________

3:6-14, 20 ________________________________

4:30-31 ________________________________

5:7-9 ________________________________

7:9 ________________________________

13:26-27 ________________________________

16:1-13 (esp. 1-4, 9) ________________________________

23:10-14 ________________________________

2. To understand why adultery is a fitting picture of apostasy, carefully consider this question: What do the following passages teach about marriage (all were written prior to Jeremiah's day and thus were a part of Jeremiah's heritage)?

Genesis 1:27 (Note the close connection between *male and female* and *the image of God.*)

Genesis 2:18-25 (Is the expression of sexuality sinful? How many people are essential for marriage? What is to happen to relationships between a son and his parents when the son is married? What does this tell us about the quality and character of marriage?)

Exodus 20:14 (Consult a dictionary concerning the definitions of *adultery* and *fornication.*)

Leviticus 20:10-21; Deuteronomy 22:13-30 (Summarize God's attitude toward sexual sins as revealed in these passages.)

____

____

 ____

3. What do the following New Testament passages add to the Old Testament teaching?
Matthew 5:27-28
John 8:1-11
1 Corinthians 6:12-20 (Why are sexual purity and fidelity so important?)
1 Corinthians 7:1-40 (What general attitude toward marriage does Paul reveal in this long passage?)
2 Corinthians 11:2
Ephesians 5:21-33 (What are to be the relationships between (1) man and wife and (2) Christ and the church?)
Revelation 19:1-10 (Who are the bride and the bridegroom?)

4. Now, state in your own words why Jeremiah's link between adultery and apostasy is so apt.

5. C. S. Lewis said there is something so masculine about God that all else is feminine in relation to him. Is that a fair summary of the biblical view of God's relation to mankind?

6. Considering the dire consequences of adultery and apostasy (recall, for example, Lev. 20:10 and Jer. 2), what should be our attitude to them—in our own lives and in the lives of others? How should it be expressed? (Note here Jesus' teaching in Mt. 5:22 and his example in Jn. 8:1-11, also Jeremiah's example in his prophetic pronouncements.)

7. What responsibility do you have for the moral character of your community (dormitory, neighborhood, etc.)? What will you do in light of the biblical teaching?

8. Consider the character of your religious community (fellowship group, church, etc.). What will you do in the light of biblical teaching?

additional reading

"Adultery and Apostasy: The Bride and Bridegroom Theme" in The Church before the Watching World *or* The Church at the End of the 20th Century *(IVP)*

THE DISCOURAGED PROPHET 5

text:
Jeremiah 15:1-21
purposes:
1/*To better understand the humanity of Jeremiah and thus the man-nishness of man*
2/*To consider how discouragement may arise and how it may be overcome*

The lament we will reflect on in this study probably dates from the reign of Jehoiakim (609-597 B.C.), which means that Jeremiah has been prophesying for at least seventeen years. As we have seen, Jeremiah's words—and the words of the Lord—have mostly been bitter denunciations of the current social and religious scene. The future—at least the immediate future of Judah—is grim. Destruction is coming. It is in this context that Jeremiah breaks down and offers a very personal cry to the Lord.

1. To set the context for Jeremiah's lament, read 15:1-9 again. How serious is Judah's present state (vv. 1-4)? Can disaster be averted? (Note: "Though Moses and Samuel had earlier interceded successfully for sinful Israel [Ex. 32: 11-14; Nu. 14:13-24; Dt. 9:18-20, 25-29; 1 Sa. 7:5-9; 12: 19-25], they had first secured the cooperation of the nation, which Jeremiah still had not been able to accomplish"—Harrison, p. 102.)

2. What specific reason is given for the Lord's judgment (v. 4; 2 Kings 21:1-18)?

3. Verses 5-9 are a good example of the poetry in Jeremiah. How does the imagery make the message more pointed? How does the imagery enhance the "flavor" of the prophecy?

4. How is the lament of verses 10-18 a natural response on the part of Jeremiah?

5. What, according to verse 10, has been the response of the Judeans to Jeremiah's messages? Why does he mention that he has neither "lent" nor "borrowed"? Is the Judeans' response understandable? Why?

6. To curse the day of one's birth is a frequent motif in laments. Read Jeremiah's lengthier development of this motif in 20:14-18. (See also Job 3:1-26 and *Oedipus Rex*, 11. 1349-63, among many classical and Western literary texts.) This lament seems extreme; do you think it is justified in Jeremiah's case?

7. How does Jeremiah describe his past ministry (vv. 11-14)? (Note: Verse 12 probably alludes to the strength of the Babylonian armies invading from the north.)

8. What specific troubles (emotional and intellectual) has

Jeremiah experienced (vv. 15-18)? What positive reward has there been (v. 16)?

______

______

______

______

9. What is the most serious question in Jeremiah's mind (v. 18)? Jeremiah's emotional state, then, is discouragement, which is closely related to intellectual doubt. Which do you think caused which?

______

______

______

______

______

10. How does the Lord answer Jeremiah (vv. 19-21)? What does he suggest might be awry with Jeremiah's perspective (v. 19)? Notice how God encourages him by repeating a promise he gave when he first called Jeremiah as a prophet (1:18-19).

______

______

______

______

11. In whom is Jeremiah to trust, in whom not to trust (vv. 19-21)? Did the Lord honor his promise to Jeremiah? (Jeremiah lived through the fall of Jerusalem some 20 years later and died in Egypt later yet.) (Note: Throughout his life, Jeremiah's relationship to most of the people, the priests, the kings and the princes continued to be as Jeremiah described in 15:10. You may wish, for example, to read 37:1—38:28 which describes his imprisonment in graphic detail. Jeremiah's discouragement then led him to plead with Zedekiah not to return him to the cistern where he had been incarcerated. Yet Jeremiah even then refused to change his gloomy—but accurate—prophecy just for the purpose of release. He remained true to the desire of the Lord stated in 15:19 and he continued to utter "what is precious and not what is worthless.")

12. In 15:19-21 does the Lord upbraid Jeremiah for contending with him? What does this suggest about the possibility that a person can come to God in total openness, admitting his current emotional state and intellectual doubt?

13. What in the Lord's reply to Jeremiah can you take as the Lord's reply to you as you bare your own discouragement before him? What additional perspective does Jesus give in the Beatitudes (Mt. 5:11)?

additional reading

C. Stephen Evans, Despair—A Moment or a Way of Life? *(IVP)*
Elizabeth Skoglund, Loneliness *(IVP)*
C. S. Lewis, A Grief Observed *(Seabury)*

TRUE AND FALSE PROPHETS 6

texts:

Jeremiah 23:9-40; 27:1–28:17

purposes:

1/*To understand the conflict between Jeremiah and the false prophets*

2/*To begin to learn how to distinguish a true prophet from a false one in our own time*

3/*To consider how the true prophets of our time can be heard more clearly*

The book of Jeremiah gives us both examples of Jeremiah's teaching about false prophets and examples of how Jeremiah faced them in specific situations. We could study any of several sections (for example, 27:16-22 and 29:1-19), but we will look at only two in detail (23:9-40 and 28:1-17). The first section, probably dating from 605-595 B.C., is Jeremiah's *teaching* which suggests principles regarding the character and identity of false prophets. The second, dating more precisely from 594 B.C., describes one of Jeremiah's *encounters* with a false prophet—Hananiah.

1. Read Jeremiah 23:9-40. How do the false prophets identify the origin of their prophecy (23:31, 33-39)? (Note: The Hebrew word which is translated *burden* in the RSV also can mean *utterance*; Jeremiah is obviously intending here a play on words.)

2. What does Jeremiah say is the origin of false prophecy (23:13, 16, 25-28, 30, 36)?

3. What is frequently the content of the false prophets' prophecies (23:16-17; compare 8:11)?

4. Summarize the characteristics of the false prophets as given in 23:9-40. What will be their fate (vv. 12, 15, 33, 39-40)?

5. Describe Jeremiah's reaction to the presence of false prophets in Judah (23:9-11).

6. Jeremiah himself was a prophet of hope. He set his sights on the return of the Jews from exile in Babylon (not in two years as Hananiah said but in seventy years [25:12 and 29:10]) and on the coming of the Messiah as Savior and King (23:5-6). What then was false in the false prophets' message?

____

____

____

7. Implicit throughout 23:9-40 is a conception of a true prophet and the content of his prophecy. Note especially verses 18-20, 22, 28-29 and summarize their teaching concerning a true prophet.

____

____

____

____

____

8. How can one tell a true prophet from a false one? (Compare Deut. 13:1-5, 18:20-22 and Jer. 28:9; consider also the general characteristics of the false prophets Jeremiah describes in Jer. 23:9-40.) How can these considerations help us to distinguish among today's "prophets"? (Note: 1 Jn. 4:1-3 gives further guidelines for testing a "New Testament" prophet.)

____

____

9. Read Jeremiah 28:1-17. What are the dates of this series of events (28:1, 12, 17)? (Note: Zedekiah became king in 597 B.C.)

10. What was Hananiah's prophecy (28:2-4)? (Note: According to Jer. 52:28, Nebuchadnezzar had carried away 3,023 Jews in the seventh year of his reign [597 B.C.]; 832 in the eighteenth year [587 B.C.]; 745 in the twenty-third year [581 B.C.].)

11. How did Jeremiah begin his response to Hananiah (28:5-6)? Can you suggest why?

12. What was Jeremiah's reservation (28:7-8)? What does this suggest about the importance of the *continuity of tradition* or the *unity of God's continuing revelation* to the Jewish people (compare Deut. 13:1-5)? (Note: You may wish to compare here Paul's words to the church at Corinth—2 Cor. 11:4-6.)

13. How did Hananiah punctuate his prophecy and what were Jeremiah's immediate and ultimate responses (28:10-14)? (To see how Jeremiah came by the yoke-bars, see 27:1-2.)

14. How did Jeremiah punctuate his prophecy concerning Judah (28:15-16)?

15. Measure Hananiah and Jeremiah by the characteristics of true and false prophets delineated in the first half of this study. What conclusions do you reach?

16. Consider your present Christian life. Do you see where you have been led astray by believing false prophets, false teachers or misdirected leaders? How have your beliefs regarding God changed as a result of studying Jeremiah? Is this a matter of "growth" only, or had you believed a "lie," as Jeremiah might put it? List some of your *new* views, if any, and be prepared to discuss these views with the members of your study group.

17. How will you respond in light of the fact that *you* have been misled? What will you do so that others (your Christian friends, dormmates, family, etc.) will not be so misguided?

____

____

____

____

____

____

____

additional reading

J. A. Motyer, "Prophecy, Prophets," New Bible Commentary: Revised *(Eerdmans and IVP)*

J. Elliot Corbett, The Prophets on Main Street *(John Knox Press), pp. 130-32*

THE PROPHET'S WORD 7

text:
Jeremiah 36:1-32
purposes:
1/*To see how Jeremiah's prophecies were recorded and preserved*
2/*To study the responses of various individuals and groups to the words of the prophet*
3/*To consider the significance of these responses and the present implications for our own day*

This study concentrates on the importance of the word of the Lord—in terms we can all understand. Various responses to God's revealed word bring various consequences. Be alert for the consequences prophesied and the consequences that ensue.

1. Read the entire chapter and fix in mind the major events and their dates of occurrence. (Note: The fourth year of Jehoiakim would be 605/4 B.C.; the ninth month is December.)

____

____

____

2. What was Jeremiah commanded to do (v.2)? Why (v. 3)?

3. How did Baruch record the Lord's words to Jeremiah (vv. 4, 17-18)?

4. When were the words to be read (v.6)? Can you suggest any reason why this was a good time to read the words? Who was the intended audience?

5. How long did it take before a fast was proclaimed (v. 9)? (Note: This was the time when "the Babylonians overthrew Ashkelon in the plain of Philistia, an incident which probably provoked the fast"—Harrison, p. 151.)

6. How well did Baruch perform his task? Who became interested? Can you suggest why?

7. When the officials heard the scroll, how did they respond (v. 16)? Why do you suppose they felt it necessary to inform the king? What did they think his reaction would be (v. 19)? How does this passage reveal that Jeremiah was not without a few friends, even in high places?

8. What do you suppose was the purpose of the question asked in verse 17?

9. How did the king and his servants respond (vv. 23-24, 26)? Did all the court have the same reaction?

10. Was the first scroll merely replaced (vv. 27-28, 32)? Specifically how was the prophecy in the second scroll brought up to date (vv. 29-31)? What were the consequences to Jehoiakim of his response to the word of the Lord? How did his response affect Judah?

11. Compare Jehoiakim's reaction to the reading of Jeremiah's prophecy with Josiah's reaction to the reading of the newly-discovered book of the law (see 2 Kings 22:11-13 and following).

12. Why is a proper response to God's word so important? Consider each of the following passages:
Leviticus 26:3-45 (and Deut. 28:1-68)
Proverbs 1:20-33

13. Sometimes it is thought that the New Testament (more specifically, Jesus) plays down the necessity of hearing and obeying the law (or the word of the Lord). Check out this impression by reference to the following; note especially the relationship between Matthew 7:21-27 and the passages (from Lev. and Deut.) referred to above.
Matthew 7:21-27
Luke 11:27-28
John 5:24
John 8:31, 47
2 Thessalonians 1:4-10

14. Summarize the Bible's teaching concerning the significance of God's word.

15. In the light of this teaching, what changes in life will you make? Make a list here and now. Pray about your resolutions and ask the Lord for strength to obey and "continue in his word."

16. Public confession of your goals will help you strengthen your resolve. Be prepared to share them with the group and ask them to pray with you and for you. And, of course, uphold them in your prayer life too.

additional reading

Psalm 119

John W. Wenham, Christ and the Bible *(IVP)*

John R. W. Stott, The Authority of the Bible *(IVP) and* Understanding the Bible *(Regal)*

JEREMIAH THE POLITICIAN 8

texts:

Jeremiah 27–29 and 34

purposes:

1/*To see the immediate political dimensions of Jeremiah's interests*

2/*To recognize how Jeremiah was caught between a holy God whose words he was to speak and an unrighteous, unheeding nation to whom his words were addressed*

3/*To grasp the immediate political dimension of our own lives and to realize how we as Christians are to affect that dimension*

Jeremiah's early prophecy tended to concentrate on Judah's refusal to obey God in religious and moral matters. As a result of this refusal, Judah would be punished, her towns laid waste, her temple demolished, her crops destroyed. As time passed Jeremiah became more and more interested in local political affairs. As Babylon became a greater and greater threat, Jeremiah realized that it was by her that Judah was to be punished, but he also believed, for the Lord told him, that Judah's punishment would be less if it submitted peacefully to Babylonian suzerainty. We study here a few events related to this aspect of Jeremiah's life and teaching.

1. How are the events of chapter 27 dated? (Harrison specifies the date as 594 B.C. since the captivity of 597 B.C. is considered an accomplished fact; see 27:16-17.)

2. To whom is the prophecy addressed (27:3, 12, 16)? What graphic device is used (27:2)?

3. Summarize the prophecy as recorded in 27:5-15. What are the nations to do with respect to Babylon? Why (27:5-6)?

4. What is added in the prophecy addressed to the priests and the people (27:16-22)? What were the false prophets saying? (Note: The Babylonians carried away many people from Jerusalem in 597 B.C.; they took some but not all of the treasures from the temple. See 1 Kings 7:15-19 and 2 Kings 24:13.)

5. Why would Jeremiah's prophecy be discouraging to the Jews? What positive note does it contain (27:7, 11, 22)?

6. In the light of what you know of Jewish consciousness (from our studies here and otherwise) what do you imagine Jeremiah's fellow Jews thought of him? Is there any way his experience might parallel yours in this regard?

7. Reread chapter 28 to refresh your memory; then read chapter 29, a letter to the Jews taken into exile in 597 B.C. (Harrison dates this letter in 594 B.C.)

8. How did the letter get to Babylon (29:3)? Why do you suppose details like this are mentioned?

9. What is Jeremiah's advice to the exiles (29:5-7)? Why (29:10-14)? Why would the advice of 29:7 sound like treason to those left in Jerusalem? How are today's military personnel advised to act if captured?

10. What were the false prophets in Babylon saying and doing (29:23, 25-27)? What is to happen to the prophets Zedekiah, Ahab and Shemaiah (29:22, 32; see Dan. 3:19-27)?

11. Read chapter 34, which narrates events in 588 B.C. during the early stages of Babylon's final assault on Jerusalem.

12. Summarize Jeremiah's message to Zedekiah (34:2-6). Is there any hope left for Jerusalem?

13. The background to the events in 34:8-22 is not clear from the text, but commentators agree that Zedekiah emancipated the slaves in order to appease God and thus have the siege lifted. When news of an advancing Egyptian army reached the Babylonians, they regrouped to attack the Egyptians. At this point the slave owners took back their slaves. Of course, the Babylonians soon returned to their attack on Jerusalem.

14. What two charges does Jeremiah bring against the slave owners (34:13-14 and 15-16)?

15. What was the law with regard to the release of slaves (Ex. 21:2, Deut. 15:12-18)? What was the law with regard to profaning God's name (Ex. 20:7)? Are these charges strictly on religious matters? Explain.

16. What will be the result of violating these two laws

(34:17-22)? (Note: Verses 18-19 refer to "the ancient Babylonian method of ratifying a covenant [cf. Gn. 15:9f, 17], implying that those who violated the agreement could expect to meet the same end as the sacrificial animal"—Harrison, p. 147.)

17. On what note does this prophecy end?

18. Summarize Jeremiah's relation to the state (its king and princes), the people and the religious authorities as seen in chapters 27—29 and 34.

19. What principles can we see in these chapters about God's dealings with governments? What kinds of activity on the part of a prophet does God commend? What does this suggest for modern Christian activism?

additional reading

Robert Linder and Richard Pierard, Politics: A Case for Christian Action *(IVP)*
Wesley Pippert, Memo for 1976 *(IVP)*
John B. Anderson, Between Two Worlds: A Congressman's Choice *(Zondervan) and* Congress and Conscience *(Lippincott)*
Mark Hatfield, Conflict and Conscience *(Word)*
Paul Henry, Politics for Evangelicals *(Judson)*
Stephen V. Monsma, The Unraveling of America *(IVP)*

ARREST AND IMPRISONMENT 9

text:

Jeremiah 37 and 38

purposes:

1/*To see the trials Jeremiah faced as the Babylonian siege of Jerusalem intensified*

2/*To grasp more fully the human dimension of Jeremiah and King Zedekiah*

3/*To see Jeremiah's life as an illustration of God's care for his servants*

Taken separately, the two accounts of Jeremiah's arrest and imprisonment contained in chapters 37 and 38 respectively are clear. Put back to back and dated as they seem to be, they are confusing. Does each chapter narrate a different event? Then why are the circumstances so similar? Is each chapter a separate telling of the same event? Then why are there so many differences? Biblical scholars do not agree on these questions, and for our purposes the answers are not essential. We will simply study both accounts and draw from each a picture of Jeremiah under extreme pressure.

1. Read chapter 37. How are the events dated (37:1)? (Harrison dates this and chapter 38 to 589-88 B.C.) What was the general reaction to Jeremiah's messages at the time of these events (37:2)? What was Jeremiah's status? What was the political situation at the time (37:4-5)?

2. Who initiated contact between Jeremiah and Zedekiah? For what purpose (37:3)? How would the events recounted in verse 5 raise a question in Zedekiah's mind? What was Jeremiah's response (37:6-10)? What do you think was Zedekiah's reaction to Jeremiah?

3. Summarize the events described in 37:11-15. (To understand Jeremiah's desire to return home [v. 12], see 32:1-15. His attempt may have been an early concern for the situation that led to the purchase of property in Anathoth.) With what was Jeremiah charged? Why might this seem reasonable? How was he punished?

4. How and why was Jeremiah released from prison (37:16-21)? What does Zedekiah's persistence in questioning

Jeremiah indicate about Zedekiah's attitude to God and his attitude to Jeremiah? What does the incident reveal about Jeremiah's attitude to God, to Zedekiah and to himself?

5. How were the false prophets put in their place (37: 19)? How do you think Jeremiah's comment on the false prophets may have affected Zedekiah's response to Jeremiah's request for "better housing"?

6. Read chapter 38. Under what circumstances was Jeremiah arrested (vv. 1-5)? What was he saying? Can you give a modern counterpart to Jeremiah's message and the response of Shephatiah, Gedaliah, Jucal and Pashhur? Who put Jeremiah in prison?

7. Describe Jeremiah's "cell" (38:6).

8. How did Jeremiah get out this time (38:7-13)? What does this tell us about Jeremiah's friends (compare 26:24; 36:19)? What was to happen to Ebed-Melech (39:15-18)? Why?

9. Who initiated the contact between Jeremiah and Zedekiah (38:14)? Why? Why would Zedekiah want Jeremiah's visit to be kept secret? How did Jeremiah bargain (38:14-16)?

10. Summarize Jeremiah's message to Zedekiah (38:17-23). Why did Zedekiah not wish to follow Jeremiah's advice?

11. How did Zedekiah bargain with Jeremiah (38:24-28)? What picture of Zedekiah emerges from these events? What was he concerned for? In comparison, how does Jeremiah stack up as a prophet and a man?

____

____

____

____

12. What do the events of chapters 37 and 38 show us about God's concern for Jerusalem? for Zedekiah? for Jeremiah? (See 1:17-19 and 15:19-21.)

____

____

____

____

13. What events in your own life have called for special perseverance on your part? on the part of your friends or close relatives? How did you react? In the light of Jeremiah 37—38, how should you react to future stressful situations?

____

____

____

____

____

14. Are there any issues (national, local or personal) on which you should now speak out and take action?

____

____

____

____

15. Are you ready to commit yourself to God in a new way, asking him to put you and keep you in the center of his will and to sustain you as that involves tough conditions? If so, why not do so now?

____

____

____

____

additional reading

Yong Choon Ahn, The Triumph of Pastor Son *(IVP)*

David Adeney, China: Christian Students Face the Revolution *(IVP)*

A RAY OF HOPE: THE NEW COVENANT 10

texts:

Jeremiah 31; Exodus 19:1-9 and 24:1-8; Hebrews 8

purposes:

1/*To examine the hope Jeremiah extended to Judah*

2/*To comprehend Jeremiah's vision of the New Covenant from his perspective*

3/*To understand how Christians today live in a fuller realization of the terms of the New Covenant*

This study focuses on the climactic—in many ways most significant—prophecy of Jeremiah's career. In what is called the Book of Consolation (chapters 30—33), Jeremiah offers two forms of hope, one immediate, one ultimate. The first involves the return of the exiles after 70 years in Babylon. The second is the establishment of the New Covenant. It is the latter which marks a watershed in Jewish religious consciousness and will form the content of this study. Because of the complexity of the issues raised here, you may wish to consult a good Bible dictionary for further information (see *New Covenant*).

1. Read Jeremiah 31. The announcement of the New Covenant (vv. 31-34) is set in the context of events which are to transpire within a century. What are those events?

---

2. List at least four characteristics of the New Covenant. First, what characteristic is described by the following: "I will put my law within them, and I will write it upon their hearts" (v. 33a)? Second, what characteristic is suggested by God's assurance, "I will be their God, and they shall be my people" (v. 33b)? Third, what characteristic is suggested by the idea that men will not learn about God from others (v.34a)? Fourth, what further characteristic is mentioned in the last half of verse 34?

3. With what previous covenant is the New Covenant contrasted? Is there any indication of when the New Covenant is to be instituted?

4. Read Exodus 19:1-9 and 24:1-8. List at least three characteristics of the Mosaic Covenant. First, what condition does it require of Israel (Ex. 19:5)? Second, what special role is played by Moses (Ex. 19:7-9)? Third, what will result if the people keep their part of the agreement (Ex. 19:

6)? How does each of these characteristics compare with those of the New Covenant?

5. Did the Israelites agree to keep their side of the bargain (Ex. 24:3)? How well did they succeed in doing so? Explain why a "new" covenant was needed to replace the "old."

6. According to the New Testament, how has the New Covenant been inaugurated (Heb.8:1-13, especially vv. 7 and 13; 1 Cor. 11:23-26; 2 Cor. 3:1-18)? In what sense is the New Covenant associated with gradual Christian maturity (2 Cor. 3:18)?

7. Read R. K. Harrison's "Additional Note on the New Covenant" at the end of this study. What light does it throw on the answers to questions 2-6 above?

8. Refer again to Jeremiah 31:31-34. How many of the characteristics of the new relationship established by the New Covenant are present now in God's relationship with you? What characteristics of this covenant seem to have become operative in God's relationships with other Christians living today? Are any missing? For example, do we need teaching in the church today or does each Christian so know God directly that no teaching is required? Do Christians act as if God had written his law on their hearts? Do you? What hope, then, is offered for the future?

9. How will your increased knowledge of the New Covenant influence your (a) prayer life, (b) ethical understanding, (c) sense of forgiveness of sins?

additional reading

J. Murray, "Covenant," New Bible Dictionary *(Eerdmans), pp. 264-68*

F. F. Bruce, The Epistle to the Hebrews *(Eerdmans), pp. 168-80*

additional note on the new covenant

The prophecy of Jeremiah marks a watershed in Hebrew religious and cultic life. From this point onwards there is a significant divergence between what has obtained in the past and what will characterize the future religious observances of Israel. Undergirding the whole of national life, and giving specification to Israel as the Chosen People, was the covenant relationship which had been established at Sinai. Basic to this agreement was the obligation of the Israelites to obey the divine stipulations, a situation familiar to them from their acquaintance with second-millennium BC secular international treaties. During the Settlement period, however, the allurements of pagan Canaanite religion succeeded in wooing away the allegiance of the Israelites from their covenantal responsibilities. This departure constituted in effect the apostasy which, in an even more developed form, the pre-exilic prophets were to condemn so resolutely.

Part of the difficulty lay in the fact that a degree of compromise had been reached between the practice of covenantal religion and indulgence in the corrupt, depraved rites of Canaanite worship by a process of religious syncretism. Consequently pagan forms were assimilated into traditional Hebrew worship, so that at most periods in pre-exilic Israelite history the resultant blend could be said to bear some superficial resemblance to orthodox worship.

However, when the situation was examined more closely it became obvious that the pervasive immoral rituals of Canaan were completely dominant in the minds of the majority of worshippers. Not unnaturally this led to an advanced degree of popular enthusiasm for religion, but what apparently escaped the notice of generations of Israelites was that the Canaanite prostitute . . . had nothing in common at any level with the demands of an ethical deity for a life to be pursued in terms of holiness. . . . The typical Near Eastern pattern of living according to personal inclination or the traditions of one's ancestors and in independence of codified law persuaded many generations of Hebrews that the ways of their fathers were suitable for them to follow also.

In his proclamation of judgment and doom upon the nation as a punishment for apostasy and wilful sin, Jeremiah was reminding his reluctant and hostile hearers that they had consistently disregarded the obligations of the Sinai covenant. The moral and ethical nature of God demanded that His rights in the covenant agreement be observed, and when the situation took a far different turn it merely followed that punishment for Israel was in fact a manifestation of divine justice. Jeremiah saw that the Mosaic covenant had been deficient even at its best because it had been imposed externally, much as the international treaties of the day were. Although it involved a comprehensive sacrificial system for the removal of sin, it still did not provide for the forgiveness of iniquity committed deliberately and with premeditation (Nu. 15:30). Sins which issued from this kind of obduracy found their highest form of development in the deliberate rejection of covenant love. . . . Since this had been the pattern of Israelite life for many centuries it was clearly of great importance for fresh provision to be made for future generations, so that the lessons of spirituality to be learned from the experiences of captivity could be implemented in the process of subsequent national renewal.

The new covenant contemplated by Jeremiah would be one of the spirit rather than the letter (cf. 2 Cor. 3:6), and as a response to divine mercy . . . would spring freely from the depths of man's being. The offer by God of forgiveness and reconciliation would result in a deep surge of gratitude from the penitent Israelites, and a fuller awareness of the obligations of spiritual fellowship with God. Moses had been the means by which a glorious external covenant had been established with Israel. That this agreement had proved ineffective over the centuries was much more of a reflection upon the faults of the Israelites themselves than upon the nature of the covenant. Nevertheless, the progressively deteriorating nature of the situation involving the relationship at all levels had rendered the Sinai agreement ineffectual, and it was left to Jeremiah to proclaim the advent of a new covenant with the Israelites. Because allegiance to this covenant would be motivated internally, it would be of permanent validity and duration for the people. While the new agreement would be made with the Israelites, it would not be restricted to them, for because of the essential freedom of choice which it posited it would ultimately be operative between any willing person and God.

In acclaiming this new form of covenantal relationship both Jeremiah and Ezekiel saw that it changed the older concept of a corporate relationship completely by substituting the individual for the nation as a whole. One immediate corollary of this situation was that a man could no longer blame his misconduct upon inherited traditions or current social tendencies. Instead, under the new covenant he would have to accept personal responsibility for his own misdeeds. Probably the most significant contribution which Jeremiah made to religious thought was inherent in his insistence that the new covenant involved a one-to-one relationship of the spirit. When the new covenant was inaugurated by the atoning work of Jesus Christ on Calvary, this important development of personal, as opposed to corporate faith and spirituality was made real for the whole of mankind. Henceforward anyone who submitted himself consciously in faith to the person of Christ as Saviour and Lord could claim and receive membership in the church of God. The new covenant in the blood of Christ, therefore, is the fruition of God's sovereign grace, conveying through a specifically spiritual relationship an adequate provision for the forgiveness of all sin, a more profound experience of divine mercy as a result of such forgiveness, and a wider sense of brotherhood among men by virtue of membership in the fellowship of Christ.—R. K. Harrison, *Jeremiah and Lamentations* (IVP), pp. 138-40.

THE FALL OF JERUSALEM 11

text:
Jeremiah 39:1-14; 40:1-6; 52:1-30 and Lamentations 4
purposes:
1/*To grasp the facts surrounding the fall of Jerusalem*
2/*To understand the human significance of the devastation of this great city*
3/*To reflect on the modern significance of the fall of Jerusalem*

We will first consider the reported facts about the fall of Jerusalem (587 B.C.) and then see how Lamentations sets those facts in emotional and theological perspective. Since most of our attention will focus on the latter, we will not linger over the description of the destruction, but proceed quickly to its human and divine significance. Lamentations may have been written by Jeremiah. Tradition so attributes it, but the question of authorship is unresolved. Many scholars, however, believe that the author was an eyewitness of the fall of Jerusalem.

1. Read Jeremiah 39:1-10 and 52:1-30. (Note: 39:15-18 belongs logically after 38:28.)

2. How long was the heavy siege of Jerusalem? (Note: The ninth year, tenth month is January 588 B.C.; the eleventh year, fourth month is July 587 B.C.)

3. Summarize the events in 39:1-14 and 52:1-27. What happened to the city, the temple, the palace, the people, the king, his sons, the nobles? Who was left in Jerusalem?

4. Read 39:11-14 and 40:1-6. What treatment did Jeremiah receive? Why? What did Jeremiah decide to do?

5. Read slowly and thoughtfully the poetic lament of Lamentations 4. Then reread verses 1-12 which describe in vivid imagery the effects of the siege and fall of Jerusalem.

6. List the details on which the poet focuses in 4:1-12. What has happened to the rich? to the mothers and children? to the starving and the slain? to the fleeing, among whom is the king (4:18-20 the "Lord's anointed")? How does the poet make us "feel" the devastation?

7. How expected was such devastation (4:12)? Why do you suppose the poet inserts the hyperbole of the verse?

8. Why did the destruction come (4:13)? What special punishment did the false prophets and apostate priests have (4:14-16)?

9. Where did Judah expect help (4:17)? (Recall earlier studies.)

10. Lest Judah's neighbors rejoice in her fall, the poet adds verses 21-22. How do these verses both indicate a furtherance of God's justice and a trust in his mercy?

11. What perspective does Lamentations add to the chronicle of Jeremiah 39:1-14 and 52:1-30?

12. What light do you think Lamentations sheds on our understanding of God's ways with man today?

13. Do you think that knowing God's favored city has been destroyed can help us as Christians? Explain.

14. Where do you feel God wants you to invest your energies in today's unstable world?

additional reading

John W. Wenham, The Goodness of God *(IVP)*
Francis A. Schaeffer, Death in the City *(IVP)*

JEREMIAH IN EGYPT 12

text:

Jeremiah 42–44

purposes:

1/*To trace the final events in Jeremiah's life*

2/*To consider the way God guides his people*

3/*To reflect on the life of Jeremiah as a model for a Christian's life today*

After the fall of Jerusalem (587 B.C.), Jeremiah chose to stay with the remnant in Palestine rather than to go with the exiles to Babylon. But things went very badly for those who remained (see Jer. 40—42). Within two months Gedeliah, whom Nebuchadnezzar appointed governor of the remnant, was treacherously slain by Ishmael; so were a large number of other Jews. Johanan, who entered the narrative as a savior, forced Ishmael to flee. This left Johanan in charge of the diminished, weak, impoverished and frightened group of Jews who then gathered at a village near Bethlehem. Afraid of the Babylonians (because the governor appointed by Nebuchadnezzar had been slain by a Jew) and too weak to stand alone and construct a viable existence on their own (they were, after all, not considered worth taking as captives), they approached Jeremiah for advice. The present study traces the course of events from this point to the close of the historical section of the book. It focuses on the spiritual obduracy of the Jewish remnant.

1. Read Jeremiah 42—43:1-7. In 42:1-6, who asks Jeremiah for advice? What specifically are they concerned for? What is Jeremiah's reaction? How anxious to follow God's leading do they appear to be?

____

____

____

____

____

____

2. How long does it take for Jeremiah to reply (42:7)? Can you suggest why? Do you see any practical implication for your own attitude about God's leading?

____

____

____

____

____

____

____

3. To whom does Jeremiah reply (42:8)? What is God's answer to the remnant's question (42:9-22)? Is there any hesitancy about it? What does it mean for God to "repent" of the evil done to Judah (42:10; see 18:1-12)? How do God's words through Jeremiah counter the Jews' fear of the Babylonians (42:11-12)? How do verses 18-22 suggest that Jeremiah knows what their answer will be?

4. Who responds to Jeremiah's counsel (43:1-4)? What do they decide? What reason do they give? Can you suggest any further and perhaps more likely reason? What in your own experience parallels such action?

5. Who goes to Egypt? Why do most commentators feel that Jeremiah did not go willingly (43:5)?

6. Read Jeremiah 43:8—44:30. Jeremiah's prophetic activity does not end after he gets to Egypt. What two subjects does it concern (43:8-13 and 44:1-30)?

7. What does Jeremiah prophesy about Egypt (43:8-13)? How does this square with his warning to the Jews before they came to Egypt? In what way is Jeremiah's method here like that which he has used previously? (Note: Nebuchadnezzar's invasion of Egypt in about 568 B.C. was "more of a punitive expedition than a wholesale reduction of the land" —Harrison, p.166.)

8. What is the substance of Jeremiah's prophecy concerning the Jews in Egypt? In what way were the Jews continuing to offend God (44:8-10)? What were the consequences to be (44:11-14)?

____

____

____

____

9. Who answers Jeremiah's charge (44:15-19)? How do they answer it? Who is responsible for the apostate behavior?

____

____

____

____

10. In the face of alternate explanation of the same state of affairs (in this case the disastrous events in Jewish history from 609-580 B.C.), how can one decide which explanation is more likely to be true? Why should the Jews have recognized that Jeremiah was speaking the truth? On what basis does Jeremiah argue that the Jews are wrong (44:20-23)? (Note: First he argues from past events; then he argues from events about to unfold. Jeremiah's prophecy is thus checkable, falsifiable. Harrison says that after Hophra's "Libyan campaign of 569 BC a young relative, Ahmose, was proclaimed pharaoh in a revolt. Hophra tried to defeat Ahmose in battle in 566 BC, but was slain, as Jeremiah had prophesied"—p. 169.)

 ____

11. The actions of the Jews in chapters 42—43 could be chalked up to spiritual obstinacy. What might explain that condition? Do you find it reflected in your own life? From your study in Jeremiah, what, if anything, is the cure?

12. Think back over the key events in Jeremiah's life. List some of them. How might Jeremiah and his actions be a model for your approach to life in a society crumbling from spiritual and moral rot? Be specific and be prepared to talk about your conclusions.

additional reading

J. A. Motyer, The Day of the Lion: The Message of Amos *(IVP)*

NOTES FOR THE LEADER

Prepare each study by first working through the questions each participant is to answer. This will give you a good idea of what problems may have arisen in the participants' minds as they prepared the study. Make a list of questions you still have concerning the material. Only after you have worked completely through the study should you read any further in these notes.

After working through the questions, read through the following notes, each of which relates to a question or set of questions. Some of your own difficulties may thus be cleared up. Those which remain can be checked out by reference to standard Bible study aids such as R. K. Harrison, Jeremiah and Lamentations *(IVP),* The New Bible Commentary: Revised *(Eerdmans and IVP) or* The New Bible Dictionary *(Eerdmans). Jeremiah poses some rather tough problems and scholars disagree on some points. So don't expect to have all your questions totally resolved. Still, with the passages we will study there should be few unresolvable problems of serious consequence.*

THE PROPHET'S CALL 1

Have you worked through the study? If not, stop reading. Do the study.

Ready now? Okay. The purpose of this study, from the standpoint of the whole group and you as leader, should be (1) to get into the life and times of Jeremiah with as much zest as the difficulty of the material will allow and (2) to challenge each member with the fact that God speaks to individuals as well as groups and nations such as Judah. The opening chapter of Jeremiah is exciting reading. It shows at least a glimpse of Jeremiah the man or Jeremiah the "youth," and it poses for each participant a serious personal question: How does God talk to me? Your task, then, will be to help each participant to see the drama of Jeremiah's dialogue with God and to see more clearly for himself how God is communicating with him.

Start with a prayer to this effect. Briefly set the stage for Jeremiah 1 by saying something about the general life and times of Judah in 627. See the historical notes on pages 114-16. You might also draw from 2 Kings 22—23. But do not spend more than three or four minutes. A deep historical background is not really required for the understanding of Jeremiah's call. Furthermore, the second study treats that historical context in some detail.

questions 1-2. Have someone read aloud verses 1-3. Discuss questions 1 and 2, but don't get bogged down in counting years and quibbling over dates or Jeremiah's age at the time of his call. *Youth* (v. 6) in Hebrew terms suggests someone younger than 20, but how much younger is not certain. The point of these two questions is to see that Jeremiah is a *real* man rooted in space-time history, not a mystic or guru unrelated to the external world.

question 3. Have someone read verses 4-10. The point of this question and question 6 is to bring out the fact that meaning is primarily conveyed by words and that God used words to tell Jeremiah he was to be a prophet. Francis A.

Schaeffer's comments on "propositional, verbalized revelation" are very much in order here. See especially chapters 3 and 4 in *He Is There and He Is Not Silent*. Many religious "visionaries" have only visions, uninterpreted images to guide them, but from the beginning of the Jewish nation (Gen. 12:1-3) through Moses (Ex. 3—4, for example) to Jesus Christ and the apostles (Heb. 1:1-3 and Jn. 16:13), God used *words* to convey a conception of who he is and how he wants men to act.

question 4. Some may be surprised to learn that God knows "individuals" who are yet to be born and that he has specific tasks in mind for them. This is a good time to emphasize God's loving concern for *each* person. (See also Paul's confession in Gal. 1:15-16.)

question 5. Bring out here that men's confidence is to be in God not in "maturity" or whatever else.

question 6. Note comment on question 3.

question 7. These verses divide Jeremiah's words into those of destruction and those of hope. Most of the book of Jeremiah is gloomy, but chapters 30 and 31 show that Jeremiah was ultimately a tremendous optimist. Here too is the place to point out that while God spoke *directly* to Jeremiah (how, we are not told), he spoke *through* Jeremiah to the nations, specifically Judah. Today we learn about God as the "nations" did—through the words of God's prophets, Jeremiah and the other writers of the Bible. So we have no excuse for ignorance even though God has not directly spoken to us. See here especially Hebrews 1:1-3. Your group may find it worthwhile discussing this "biblical" aspect of God's revelation to them.

questions 8-9. Have someone read verses 11-19. Here are visions "interpreted" in "words."

question 10. Jeremiah's enemies, as we will see in subsequent studies, were not just foreign invaders but even fellow Jews.

question 11. Emphasize here, as in question 5, the importance of placing one's confidence in God and not in self or in nationality, etc. (Rom. 8:31-32).

questions 12-14. These questions are designed to prompt a final sharing and should lead your group into specific prayer for each other as you seek to know more about God and his word to you through the Bible and specifically the book of Jeremiah. Paul Little's booklet *Affirming the Will of God* (IVP) might be just what someone in your group needs at this point. Why not have a few on hand to pass on to those whom it would especially benefit?

THE HISTORICAL BACKGROUND 2

This study can be optional. If your group consists of people who will study straight history for a few hours, preparing for an hour of discussion, then by all means assign this section. It provides a valuable historical perspective from which to view the life and teaching of Jeremiah.

You will note, however, that this study has only a few questions to elicit application to modern history or to personal problems today. This is by design. You will find it impossible in an hour to do more than clarify in broad outline the history of the Jewish nation from c. 716 to 587 B.C. But this is no mean accomplishment! Besides, the issues raised reappear in subsequent studies, and there will be time for their discussion then.

If you or your group insist on practical application, several such questions are listed at the end of these notes. To do justice to them as well as to the "history," double your normal discussion time, or spend two hour-long sessions on this one study.

question 1. Clarify the charts prepared by the group members. Quickly summarize the brief chronology or, if many have not prepared at all, take time to read the whole chronology. Its cursory overview is quite helpful.

question 2. Participants will probably focus on the weaknesses of the aging Hezekiah and the reformation of Manasseh. Manasseh's reformation is not mentioned in Kings, perhaps because it came late in his life and did little to change the religious life of the populace.

question 3. Have participants imagine the report Merodach-baladan took back to Babylon. This would be long remembered and pose a good reason for Babylon to pay attention to Judah when it was able to extend its empire.

questions 4-5. These questions do not require discussion; some of what they suggest will have already come out in your discussion of question 2.

questions 6-7. These can be discussed together.

questions 8-10. Brief answers will suffice.

questions 11-14. These questions focus on the seriousness with which Josiah took his task as religious reformer. Note, if no one points it out, that Josiah was already engaged in reform when the book of the law was found. God often gives more light to those who are reacting to some. Robert Munger's booklet *My Heart–Christ's Home* (IVP) shows the application of that principle in a Christian's life today.

questions 15-16. Discuss together.

question 17. This question calls for the recognition of the seriousness of sin and its consequences in space and time often far down into the future. You might point out that Jeremiah, while he lamented for the death of Josiah (2 Chron. 35:25), did not (in anything recorded in the book of Jeremiah) commend Josiah for his reforms. This suggests that, while Josiah's reforms were personally heartfelt, they may, like those of Manasseh, not have extended deeply into the lives of the people.

questions 18-20. These questions call for simple, factual answers. Do not discuss; simply answer and move on.

question 21. This is the only application question in this study. Discussing it may serve as a fitting close. It will be taken up in detail in study 6 on Jeremiah 36.

If you or your group insist on looking for more of the practical implications of the content of 2 Kings 20—23, the following suggestions may promote fruitful discussion: What parent-child relations are revealed in these chapters (note the parentage of the kings and the relative characters of fathers and sons)? Discuss the seriousness of sin: its consequences to sinner and society and subsequent events (cf. Ex. 20:5; 34:6-7; Jer. 31:29-30). Have someone summarize *My Heart–Christ's Home* (see above). What aspects of 2 Kings 20—23 are God's word to you today?

THE GREAT TEMPLE SERMON 3

Begin by praying that God will speak to each of you individually and that the four purposes of this study will be substantially fulfilled.

question l. Have someone read 26:1-3. Note that as God called Jeremiah (1:4-5), he said he would put words into Jeremiah's mouth (1:9). The Temple Sermon contains some of those words.

question 2. Notice the breadth of audience intended for the sermon. Does it include your group?

question 3. Have someone read 26:4-6. Discuss briefly.

questions 4-5, 9-10. Have 26:7-19 read by one or more people. Question 4 in group discussion can be omitted because the answer will come out in discussing question 5. Have the group list the various individuals and groups mentioned and consider, for example, why it is the priests and prophets who are primarily at odds with Jeremiah. Who was more favorable—or at least willing to listen? In considering this, your group may well need the perspective of Jeremiah 7:1-15. So you may wish to include at this point your discussion of questions 9-10. If you do, be sure that in answer to question 10 someone points out that God is interested in moral behavior—righteous thought, attitudes and action—and not in "cultic" practices that "work by being worked"; in other words, God will not be manipulated by the use of his temple as a talisman or a good luck charm. One of the reasons the Jews were so disturbed by Jeremiah's sermon is that it was based on historical precedent. Having the ark did not guarantee victory at Shiloh; in fact, the ark itself was captured. Jeremiah was saying the temple was in the same category as the ark. Subsequent history proved Jeremiah correct.

question 6. Someone is sure to bring up the question of how one can distinguish between true and false prophets, both of whom claim to speak the word of the Lord. There are a few suggestions in 26:10-19, but since this is the key issue in the following study, try to postpone the answer till then. You *could*, and depending on your group perhaps you *should*, discuss the question about modern revolutionaries. Three points can be made: (1) Modern revolutionaries tend to reject authority as such, replacing civic authority with pure personal freedom; Jeremiah submitted to the temporal authorities (as did Peter and John) but saw them as under the judgment of the eternal God (that is, they had the right to submit Jeremiah to punishment if he was guilty, but they had the responsibility to be sure that he was in fact guilty; they were not the establishers of law and order, but they were its executors). (2) Jeremiah, Peter and John were willing to take responsibility for their actions, rather than asking for amnesty or special treatment. Jeremiah was not a revolutionary but a reformer; he wished to call the Jews *back* to justice as established under Mosaic law. The system had become corrupt in practice not in essence. (A different sort of action may be necessary where the system itself has become no longer viable.) (3) All human authority is derivative; Jeremiah's prophetic word derived from God; the princes' civic authority derived from God; neither prophet nor priest, nor king, nor people, nor elder is to be taken as an absolute. When, in our political language, we begin to put a capital letter on People or President or Congress or Supreme Court, thinking them beyond judgment, we fall into unbiblical thinking. All receive their value, character, rights, authority, status and dignity from God who alone is absolute. Nonetheless, human authority is valid. The question is not whether there should or shouldn't be human authority; it is what the character of that authority is to be and whether it is conceived of as derived from the Lord of the universe and reflective of his character as expressed in Scripture.

question 7. Note the basis of the elders' argument. The elders' appeal is to God's word properly used, not to self-authority.

question 8. Handle quickly by pointing out that true prophets were not always spared and that Jeremiah was helped by friends in high places.

questions 9-10. See above.

question 12. Discuss the nature of God (the living, eternal, righteous, omniscient, omnipotent creator of the universe) in contrast to Judah's false gods.

question 14. This can be omitted in your discussion. You will probably be running out of time anyway. A brief summary will suffice.

question 15. The answer to their question will have already emerged in discussion. Briefly note the answer and move on.

question 16. Spend the remainder of your time on this one. Encourage specificity in response. What are the false gods in your culture, your church, your fellowship group, your own life? Suggestions may range from confidence in material well-being and wealth to toying with Transcendental Meditation or purely secular psychology as a solution to our personal problems. Discuss what action you should take in light of this. Try to get the participants to speak in terms they can themselves do something about. Generalizations about "our church," "our nation" or "our city" will be made, but what *exactly* will you and members of your group *do*.

ADULTERY AND APOSTASY 4

As a discussion leader you may face two problems: (1) not enough time to cover all of the passages and (2) a tendency for the group to consider only one of the two themes and to fail to sufficiently grasp their inter-connectedness. The first problem can be solved by selecting only the most important passages and questions for discussion. These are indicated in the notes to follow. The second problem will take more care. If your group can grasp the significance of Genesis 1:27 and 1 Corinthians 6:12-20 (question 2), then the relationship between the two themes should be easier to understand.

question 1. Discuss only 2:1-2; 2:20-25, 33; 4:30-31; 5:7-9; 13:26-27; and 16:1-4, 9. Divide these six sets of verses among six participants, then have each read and discuss his set in order. You will find that sexual infidelity and apostasy are so interwoven in most of these passages, that it is perhaps impossible to tell either (1) which sin is more heinous or (2) which sin is really being primarily referred to. In 16:1-4, Jeremiah is asked to picture in his own life the lack of relation between God and his people. "To the Canaanites, prosperity, defined in agricultural terms, depended on the capricious activity of Baal who could be enticed into action only by sympathetic magic. Consequently, Canaanite religion rested upon infamies such as 'sacred' prostitution in which the human act of fertility was designed as a broad hint to the god to function similarly. In Israel, prosperity found its collateral in obedience (e.g. Dt. 28; 29; Hg. 1:9-11; 2:15-19; Zc. 6:15). The moral holiness of God which rules the world requires the moral obedience of man" (*New Bible Commentary: Revised*, p. 28).

question 2. These verses, especially Genesis 1:27, show the basis for the link between adultery and apostasy. Note that man (generic: male and female) is made in God's image and that male and female seem to be aspects of that image. In other words, sexuality has its origin or basis in God; it represents something of God's nature. God is not sheer unity (as in Eastern pantheistic monism; Brahman in Hesse's *Siddhartha*, for example), but he, as we know from the New Testament, is a trinity; there were love and communication between the Father, Son and Spirit before the creation. "It is possible that the complex oneness of man and woman in marriage is also itself a reflection of the diversified unity of God . . . "(*New Bible Commentary: Revised*, p. 27). As God is unified in nature and character, so man and wife are unified in marriage. Thus to break that unity on the human level is to break the picture of the character of God. Furthermore, as God, the husband of his people, is faithful to men, so men as his bride should be faithful to him (Jer. 2: 1-2).

Not all verses in this section need to be discussed. The essential ones are Genesis 1:27 and 2:18-25 (note how fidelity is important in the institution of marriage) and Leviticus 20:10-21 (the key idea to note here is the seriousness of sexual sin). In Leviticus 20:10-21 and Deuteronomy 22:13-30, you may wish to discuss the various kinds of sexual sins; some participants may be surprised at the moral stance of the Mosaic law (given by God).

question 3. Concentrate on Matthew 5:27-28 to note that Jesus extends the definition of immorality to inner thoughts and attitudes; on John 8:1-11 to see how Jesus both extends the application of the law to the woman's accusers and then forgives her and tells her to sin no more; on 1 Corinthians 6:12-20 to see the New Testament version of Genesis 1:27 discussed above; on 2 Corinthians 11:2 to see the clear expression of the relationship of the church to God. The other verses add depth and detail, but you will not have time to discuss them, if you are limited to an hour.

question 4. Be brief here. The idea should be clear by now.

questions 5-6. Answers will have already come up in previous discussion.

 questions 7-8. Handle each in turn. These are action-motivating questions and should help participants bring the material into their own lives.

THE DISCOURAGED PROPHET 5

This passage is rich but straightforward, and should pose few difficulties.

questions 1-3. These do not need discussion. Begin with question 4.

question 4. Have someone read 15:1-9 aloud. Focus on the "hard" words Jeremiah had to speak, how few words of encouragement he could utter and what reception this message would naturally receive.

question 5. The negative reaction to Jeremiah was based solely on the message he brought, not on his business dealings.

question 6. Have someone read 20:14-18. Summarize Job's lament in 3:1-26. If someone is familiar with *Oedipus Rex*, have him explain the lament in that context.

question 7. This is background for the crucial questions of this study—questions 8-11, on which you should encourage deep discussion.

question 10. Note the Lord's promise and the condition for it. God does not treat Jeremiah as a puppet. He, like the people of Jerusalem, can choose to be faithful or he can go his own way. Notice also that the Lord returns to the same language he used when he called Jeremiah over seventeen years before.

question 11. After discussing the questions, have someone summarize Jeremiah 37:1—38:28 and how Jeremiah handled a discouraging situation then—by pleading not to be put back in the wretched cistern.

question 12. God uses strong language in 15:9 and suggests that Jeremiah has uttered worthless words (perhaps some of those in 15:15-18), but he does not want Jeremiah to bottle up his doubts. By baring them openly before God,

God can reply and restore Jeremiah's confidence.
question 13. Some participants may wish God would speak to them as he spoke to Jeremiah. Encourage them to see that he is doing so *through* Jeremiah. Furthermore, we today have the word of the Lord Jesus and much of it is very encouraging indeed. See the Beatitudes, Matthew 5:1-11.

TRUE AND FALSE PROPHETS 6

This discussion is likely to be spirited. Few topics are of more continued relevance than how to know that what you know is truly so. That is, what is sound authority? In a time of religious pluralism, such as ours, the question is of supreme importance.

One way to begin the discussion is to read from a popular pundit who proposes a solution to one or more of today's social ills. At the time of this writing, Timothy Leary, Alan Watts, George Leonard, B. F. Skinner, Herbert Marcuse and Alvin Toffler were a few of the prophetic voices being heard in the U.S. It should be easy for you to update the list. But be sure you really understand whatever you choose to read; do not misrepresent what the "prophet" is in fact saying. Harrison's note on true and false prophets is especially helpful (Harrison, pp. 122-23).
question 1. Have one or more of the participants read aloud chapter 23. This question is designed to show that false prophets identify themselves in the same way as true prophets, thus the problem for the rest of us.
question 2. Essentially false prophecy is pure humanism; the message is spun from men's imaginations. The true prophet receives his message from God. One of the ways to evaluate a modern prophet is to ask him *where* his ideas come from and *why* he thinks they are true.
question 3. False prophets tend to preach the easy message, the one people like to hear—peace, not war; prosperity, not judgment. (See, for example, Hananiah's prophecy

in 28:2-4.) Many modern prophets who ought to know better are optimistic in spite of themselves (Alvin Toffler in *Future Shock*, for example).

questions 4-6. These questions cause much comment, but they do not advance the major purposes of this study, so try to move the group quickly on to questions 7-9.

questions 7-8. These and question 9 are the crux of the study. Jeremiah's message—and that of all true prophets—must speak to the reality of man's situation in society and before God. Men are fallen and have sinned; there will be judgment. Even the false prophets are involved in moral turpitude. All of Judah is deeply immersed in sin (as we saw in last week's study) and must repent if judgment is to be mitigated (7:5-7). Even so, Jeremiah knows that Nebuchadnezzar will capture Judah. Destruction of Jerusalem can be prevented if Judah will repent of her sins and give in to the Babylonians, but the capture cannot be prevented (21:1-10). In other words, judgment must come. These are hard words (23:19-20, 29), but they are true. The Scripture is not just religiously true but true to the reality that is there. The true prophet, therefore, is one who tells the truth regardless of how unpleasant it is. A person who tells us our problems can be solved by self-affirmation (I'm OK, you're OK), or by drug therapy, or by sociological or behavioral engineering, or by returning to an unconditioned, natural state—but who fails to see these solutions in relation to the concept of a righteous, holy God and a fallen, sinful humanity—is misleading us, even though there may otherwise be some validity to his proposal.

questions 9 and 13. In short, there are three criteria for a true prophet: (1) He must prophesy in the name of the Lord; (2) what he says must come true; and (3) he must stand in the tradition of the prophets who prophesied in the name of the God of Abraham, Isaac and Jacob, that is, his teaching must square with God's past revelation in Scripture. In other words, doctrine is vital: It is *the most important* test of a true prophet.

Your time may be about to expire at this point. And, rather than ending here or one or two questions later, skip to question 13. Be sure the group discusses the necessity for *continuity of tradition*. God is the one true God. He does not change. If he reveals himself to be *such and such* at one time and place, he *is* in fact what he has revealed himself to be. God does not lie; he cannot lie (1 Sam. 15:29) about himself or about us. In other words, the continuity of God's message to man must be maintained if God is to be the *true* God speaking *truly* and if revelation is to be his word.

In the New Testament (1 Jn. 4:1-3), we are told that a false prophet can be identified primarily on the basis of what he believes about Jesus Christ. What, then, do some contemporary prophets say about Christ? That he is a good man, or a good example, or a good teacher? That's not enough. That he is God incarnate: This alone will do. If, then, a prophet fails this test he is to be treated as a man, true, but he is to be listened to with great caution.

questions 10-12, 15-16. Discuss only if there is sufficient time.

questions 17-18. Have the participants share their answers to these questions.

You might close the discussion by asking how they would evaluate the following advice by Rick Chapman in *How to Choose a Guru* (Harper and Row), p. 5: "Follow your nose through the lives of the great saints and Masters throughout history. . . . Here are the names of some that you can't go wrong with: Zoroaster, Rama, Krishna, Buddha, Jesus, Mohammed, Meher Baba. . . ." Or you might close by reading J. Elliot Corbett's modernization of Jeremiah 23:13-14 in *The Prophets on Main Street* (John Knox Press), pp. 130-32.

THE PROPHET'S WORD 7

The main point of this study is that God demands that men pay attention to his word, for he speaks truly and holds men responsible not only for hearing his word but for bringing their lives into accord with it.

questions 1-2. Let the group get the sequence of events clearly in mind.

question 3. This passage is one of the Old Testament's few indications of how its materials were first recorded. Harrison comments: "Ancient Hebrew books had their text written in parallel columns, necessitating the unrolling of the scroll as the reading proceeded. The actual contents of the document in question are unknown, though it probably comprised an anthology of material proclaimed between 626 and 605 BC" (p. 150). Material in the first twenty chapters of Jeremiah would appear to be closely related to that in the first scroll, but the exact contents of either the first or second scroll cannot be certainly known.

questions 4-5. Note the extent of Jeremiah's intended audience.

questions 6-7. Encourage the group to see the drama of these events. Why was the situation so intense?

question 8. The officials wanted to know just how authoritative this scroll was. Apparently they had considerable respect for Jeremiah. But they wanted to be sure before they took the scroll to the king.

question 9. Note that the king's impudence startled and frightened the officials who brought the scroll. Why?

questions 10-11. Note that while the people were ready followers of one king's religious laxity, they were not so ready to follow a former king's piety. Josiah's reforms were imposed from the top down, and, while they postponed God's judgment, they did not go deeply enough to effect culture-deep reformation.

question 12. Divide the group into three and give each section a chance to review these passages. Ask each section to have one person summarize for the whole group the consequences of obeying or not obeying God's word.

questions 13-14. Divide the group into five and have one person from each section summarize the point of each passage. These verses are, of course, lifted from their context, but not violently. Note how knowing/obeying God's word is simply and flatly a matter of life and death. This point is universal throughout the Old and New Testaments. In fact, it illustrates how Jeremiah in this one point stands in the tradition of the prophets as every true prophet is required to do (see study 5 and Deut. 13:1-5).

questions 15-16. Focus the group's attention on their own response to God's word. Ask if anyone has anything to share concerning his own changed or changing attitudes to God's word. The Scripture contains many helpful meditations on the existential vitality of God's word. Your group might pray together the words of Psalm 119:11.

JEREMIAH THE POLITICIAN 8

This lesson should be related as closely as possible to political events unfolding at the time your group conducts this study. As the leader, you should try to link various aspects of Jeremiah's situation to your country's politics. At the time this study was first used, Spiro Agnew had just resigned as Vice-President, the Senate Watergate hearings were in mid-course, the war in Southeast Asia was still in progress and Israel and the Arab nations were again at war. Seldom does one find a Jeremiah standing forth in all of this. Your group might well consider whether one seems to be appearing now.

One exemplary prophetic utterance was given by Mark Hatfield at the Presidential Prayer Breakfast in Washington in early 1973. A relevant portion is reproduced in *Memo for 1976* by Wesley Pippert (IVP), page 20. Be alert for statements like this and have your group share their own knowledge of concerned Christian action in politics today.

questions 1-5. By this time Jeremiah is convinced that Babylon will conquer the whole area—Judah and its neighbors. If the people do not resist they will be able to live on their land, in captivity but in peace. If they resist their cities will be sacked, the land laid waste, the local residents killed or exiled. If they are exiled and live in peace, they will return. Note the *conditional* nature of all this prophecy.

question 6. Relate Jeremiah's situation (he was thought by many to be a traitor) to yours or that of a Christian who acts and speaks prophetically in today's world. Have the group be specific concerning political situations you face.

questions 7-8. The record of Jeremiah's prophecy is rooted in space-time history. This is not just a "religious" story with a "moral."

question 9. This question may have already been considered in discussing questions 3-5.

question 10. Note the seriousness of being a false prophet. What caution should that be to energetic Christians with political interests?

questions 11-17. Chapter 34 adds a dimension to our understanding of Jeremiah as a politician, for here we see him decrying the way Jewish slaves were being treated. The Mosaic law was violated in two ways—once by the unjust treatment of slaves and again by the breaking of an agreement. Furthermore, the seriousness of these breaches of the law is made unmistakably clear. Nonetheless, these questions can be omitted if you find there is not time.

questions 18-19. Be sure to save plenty of time for these key questions of implication and application. Close in prayer focused on your own role in current political affairs.

ARREST AND IMPRISONMENT 9

If your group has a limited time, you may wish to discuss only chapter 38 (of the two chapters it seems to raise the more interesting and relevant issues); in that case start with question 6.

questions 1-2. Zedekiah vacillated remarkably. Since help from Egypt seemed on its way, his hopes were raised.

Perhaps he wanted Jeremiah to confirm his hope by changing his prophecy from certain doom by the hands of the Babylonians to salvation from Egypt. Since Jeremiah's message remained constant, Zedekiah must have been terribly disappointed. Yet he did not really seek to silence Jeremiah. Apparently Zedekiah highly respected Jeremiah; perhaps he feared him. In any case, he did not attempt to do away with him. Have the group examine the nature of Jeremiah's relationship to Zedekiah along such lines as the above.

question 3. Your group may wish to consider why (since he was certain of Judah's doom) Jeremiah painstakingly consummated the purchase of property which would never really be his to hold. Most commentators believe this was a sign of Jeremiah's ultimate hopes for God's people.

questions 4-5. Again it appears that Zedekiah was weak personally, unable to hold firmly the reins of state, unwilling to commit his paths to the Lord, blown about by requests from his court counsellors. Contrast this with Jeremiah, but note the strength of Jeremiah's request (v. 20).

question 6. The prince's basic complaint was that Jeremiah was demoralizing the soldiers and thus harming the people in general—a typical charge against those seeking peace in a time of war. Compare the charge against the Vietnam peace movement in the U.S. in the late 60s. Note that Zedekiah "let" the princes have their way, thus further indicating his own weaknesses.

question 7. "Most houses in Jerusalem had private cisterns (cf. 2 Ki. 18:31; Pr. 5:15) for storing water collected from rainfall or from a spring. They were usually pear-shaped with a small opening at the top, which could be covered over if necessary to prevent accidents or contamination of the water. By 1200 BC cisterns were lined with cement, a practice illustrated by the Qumran reservoirs. The cistern in question was apparently not in use, but nevertheless contained a residue of tacky mud in which the prophet was compelled to stand or sit" (Harrison, p. 155).

Someone in your group may be familiar with cisterns in use today. Some of them are rather like the ones in Jerusalem 2500 years ago.

question 8. Jeremiah had a number of very good friends. See, for example, how Baruch was to fare (45:1-5).

questions 9-10. Zedekiah appears to have feared both the war party in Jerusalem (thus he saw Jeremiah privately) and the Jews who had already submitted to Babylon. Moreover his constant reversion to Jeremiah's counsel suggests he feared Jeremiah as well. Perhaps Jeremiah's accuracy in predicting disaster made him more aware that he should have accepted Jeremiah's counsel much earlier. Yet he did not have either the strength or integrity to stand against his "princes."

question 11. Jeremiah gives in to Zedekiah's somewhat deceitful proposal. Consider whether that means Jeremiah's own strength of purpose may be failing him. Still, note that Jeremiah's word from the Lord remains constant.

questions 12-15. These are "significance" and "application" questions. Leave plenty of time for sharing. Ask members to share any hard situations they are facing; close in praying for each other as you come up against known or unknown trials.

A RAY OF HOPE 10

This study raises some most complex issues: How does God establish his relations with man? Do these relationships change? How? Why? In what ways does God now relate to us? One of the basic ways the Bible answers these questions is in its recording and explanation of the covenants. Some theologians single out six separate but closely related covenants: the pre-deluvian Noahic (Gen. 6:18-21); the post-deluvian Noahic (Gen. 9:9-17); the Abrahamic (Gen. 15: 1-17; 17:1-21); the Mosaic (Ex. 19:1-9; 24:1-8); the Davidic (Ps. 89; 132); the New Covenant (Jer. 31:31-34; Ezek. 37:

26-28; Mt. 26:28; 1 Cor. 11:23-26; 2 Cor. 3:1-8; Gal. 3: 15-18; Heb. 8—10). The first five are all various manifestations of the Old Covenant (from which concept the Old Testament is named). The New Covenant, announced by Jeremiah (probably just before or after the destruction of Jerusalem in 587 B.C.) and Ezekiel, was inaugurated five hundred years later by Jesus Christ. In a real sense the entire New Testament is an exegesis of the terms of that covenant. Christians today participate, if not wholly at least potentially, in its terms.

In its generic sense a *covenant* is an agreement between two parties: There are terms and conditions and certain sanctions for breaking. In the Bible a *covenant* is an agreement or engagement established by God; it is not prefaced by any bargaining with man.

question 1. Do not linger on the answer to this one. Simply establish that the announcement of the New Covenant is set in the context of the prophecy of the return of the Jews to Palestine and specifically to Jerusalem.

question 2. The New Covenant has these basic characteristics: (1) It is *internal*; God's law has been internalized and has become a matter of the spirit rather than the letter (v. 33); (2) it establishes a community of people under God (v. 33); (3) it involves a *direct* personal relation, no intermediary or teacher or guru, between God and each man (high or low; leader or follower) (v. 34); (4) it involves a total forgiveness of man's sin (v. 34) and thus does not require constant sacrifices. These are rich concepts, and your group may wish to spend considerable time in discussing each one.

question 3. The New Covenant is contrasted with the Mosaic covenant. Jeremiah gives no indication of when it will be instituted; for that we need the witness of the New Testament.

question 4. The Mosaic covenant bears the following characteristics: (1) It requires obedience to God's voice, his Law or Word; (2) it involves an intermediary—Moses; (3) the Jews will be God's special "people"—implying primarily a corporate rather than individual and personal relationship to God. Some theologians insist that the requirement of obedience is not intended to suggest a covenant of works rather than of faith; they point to the prior covenant with Abraham where the conditions were more obviously faith-oriented. See Genesis 15:1-6 and Hebrews 11:8-12. In terms of contrast with the New, the Old Covenant is external, mediated by teaching from the law (Deut. 6:4-8) and by Moses, corporate, and accompanied by constant sacrifices.

question 5. The history of the Jews in the Old Testament provides the answer. The need for God's standards to be internalized in man is apparent. To really be in concord with God a man needs a new heart, a new nature.

question 6. Divide these passages among the members and have three people report their findings. Hebrews indicates that the New Covenant is now operative; 1 Corinthians 11 equates Jesus' death with the inauguration of the New Covenant; 2 Corinthians 3 indicates that Christians are under this covenant but that there is growth and development in its realization in each believer.

question 7. Those who have prepared beforehand will probably have incorporated the material from Harrison's commentary on Jeremiah into their answers to the above. So this question can be bypassed.

question 8. Take each characteristic in turn and ask the group to comment. The New Covenant in Jeremiah's terms seems closer to fulfillment after Jesus' death and resurrection and after the coming of the Holy Spirit, but we await the full internalization of God's standards in our hearts and the perfect obedience and community that will ensue. And, while each Christian can know God personally, we still benefit from having other men teaching us about God. Our hope is for complete fulfillment of the promise in the full life with God in his eternal city.

question 9. This is a good time to share your personal hopes and aspirations and get to know one another more deeply. Pray—and pray specifically—for one another as you close.

THE FALL OF JERUSALEM 11

As the group considers this key event in Jewish history, try to help them become more and more aware that for us today the fall of Jerusalem stands as a warning against naivete. Such disasters happened to Jerusalem—to God's chosen people in his chosen city—by his foreknowledge. But help them see that it could have been prevented by obedience to God's word and by continued repentance for failure to obey.

questions 1-3. The answers are straightforward and should pose no problem.

question 4. Jeremiah was given deferential treatment probably because the Babylonians feared and respected him. He must have appeared to them to be on their side; with that many Jews would have agreed. In any case, the Babylonians were not about to offend a man of such consummate foresight and possible danger, for who could predict what a proven prophet might be capable of?

question 5. Have one especially good reader in your group read Lamentations 4 meaningfully. (You may want to ask him ahead of time so he can look it over in advance.)

question 6. Answers to these questions also answer question 11. The poet sees the destruction of Jerusalem as an insider—one who feels deeply and conveys the shape of the experience of catastrophe.

question 7. Several verses in Lamentations 4 are ironic. No one in Jerusalem could imagine anyone anywhere thinking Jerusalem could fall. They should have told the Babylonians! Somehow they never got the word.

question 8. Verse 13 gives the spiritual reason for Jerusalem's destruction. The false prophets were cut off from both God and the people. The seers had become blind—

again the irony of the poet.
question 9. Egypt is intended.
question 10. More irony, as the poet taunts Edom and warns her not to gloat; her turn is coming!
questions 12-13. See the comment opening the leader's notes to this study.

JEREMIAH IN EGYPT 12

Since this is the final study, you might begin by briefly listing the major events and themes you have covered in the twelve studies. This may help to fix in each participant's consciousness the personal relevance of Jeremiah.
question 1. First, have one of the members summarize the action recounted in Jeremiah 40—41. Then handle the questions listed. Note throughout this chapter the commitment of the total remnant. Except for Jeremiah and Baruch they all seem of one mind.
question 2. Jeremiah was not one to react hastily (see Jer. 28, especially vv. 10-17). He probably wanted to be absolutely sure his message was God's message. Of course, it was one totally consistent with Jeremiah's past evaluation of Babylon and Egypt. You may wish to discuss (1) our tendency to rush in and give others our counsel long before we understand the situation and (2) our anxiety to get an immediate answer to guidance questions in our own lives.
questions 3-4. We all have a tendency to ask God for guidance, claim to be fully open to his leading and then go our own way anyway: "God, I want to go your way on this one; just tell me what to do. But bless me as I do my own thing!" How much of our own lifestyle boils down to that? Jeremiah 18:1-10 is an excellent commentary on what it means for God to "repent"; in fact, it illuminates clearly what is called the *conditional* nature of biblical prophecy and highlights God's treatment of men as significant creatures capable of truly shaping the course of human events.

questions 5-6. The two basic topics of Jeremiah's prophecy are the future destruction of Egypt by Babylon and the future obliteration of the Jewish remnant for continued apostasy.

questions 5-7. These should be bypassed if time is limited.

question 7. A whole further study could be made of the visual nature of Jeremiah's prophecy and of God's word to Jeremiah and the Jews. See, for example, the visions of Jeremiah 1:11-19; 24:1-8 and 25:15-29 and the acted parables of 13:1-11; 16:1-4; 18:1-11; 19:1-15; 27:1—28:17; 32:1-44.

questions 8-9. Again notice the complete and knowing commitment of the remnant. The Jews had lost all faith in the one true God. Jeremiah's warning not to go to Egypt was confirmed by the totally apostate condition of those who went. His advice to go to Babylon was well borne out, for there the spiritual condition of the Jews did not sink to such depths.

question 10. We are back to the issue of how to distinguish between true and false prophecy. Recall the framework provided by study 5. How does the argument of the Jews in Egypt stack up against the three criteria listed in the notes to study 5, questions 9-13?

question 11. Discuss the importance of being open to God. He may want you to *know* more (and you think you have all the relevant facts); he may want you to *repent* (and you think you are in basic fellowship with him); he may want you to *submit* to him (and you may be holding back). Consider the fate of the Jews in Egypt as it relates to your future. Let the discussion flow freely here.

question 12. Have group members share their conclusions. Close in prayer for each other for a positive response to God's guidance.

APPENDIX A

structural outline of the book of jeremiah

During the time you are completing these studies you should plan to read the whole of Jeremiah in the order in which its text has come down to us. Unhappily, this poses a few problems, for the text appears disorganized and chaotic. It is best to begin by viewing the whole book as a collection of separate, loosely related pieces—some in prose, some in poetry. The RSV and NEB helpfully distinguish these passages. The order is not chronological, but a number of the sections are dated by reference to historical events and reigning kings. All attempts to structurally analyze the book are to some extent subjective. The following is adapted from F. Cawley and A. R. Millard in *The New Bible Commentary: Revised* (p. 628). The dates, however, derive largely from R. K. Harrison, *Jeremiah and Lamentations.*

1:1—25:38	ORACLES CONCERNING GOD'S CHOSEN PEOPLE
1:1-19	The prophet's call (626 B.C.)
2:1—6:30	The nation's summons (626-609 B.C.)
7:1—10:25	The illusions of Temple security (608 B.C.)
11:1—12:17	Jeremiah and the covenant (605 B.C. or 621 B.C.?)
13:1-27	Five warnings (c. 600-597 B.C.)
14:1—21:10	Shadow of doom (c. 600-590 B.C.)
21:11—25:38	Kings and prophets of Judah: the vision of the end (c. 597-587 B.C.)
26:1—52:34	HISTORICAL NARRATIVES
26:1-24	The reign of Jehoiakim (608 B.C.)
27:1—29:32	The prophet's common sense (c. 597-594 B.C.)
30:1—34:22	The future holds hope: the Book of Consolation (c. 589-587 B.C.)
35:1—36:32	Prophecies and events during Jehoiakim's reign (c. 605-597 B.C.)
37:1—39:18	Prophecies and events during Zedekiah's

	reign (c. 587-588 B.C.)
40:1—43:7	Prophecies and events in Judah (c. 587-586 B.C.)
43:8—44:30	Prophecies and events in Egypt (c. 585 B.C.)
45:1-5	Jeremiah's message to Baruch (c. 605 B.C.)
46:1—51:64	Prophecies against foreign nations (c. 605-585 B.C.)
52:1-34	Historical appendix

APPENDIX B

a brief chronology of judah 639-581 b.c.

639 b.c. Josiah (639-609 B.C.) at age eight comes to the throne as Judah continues its position as a nation subject to the Assyrian empire (a vassalage which began in c. 730 when Ahaz formed a treaty with Tiglath-pileser III). The capital of Assyria was Nineveh in the Tigris Valley.

c. 631 b.c. Josiah begins a reformation of religious practices continued under the reign of Manasseh (686-642 B.C.), and the hold on Judah by Assyria begins to relax as Ashurbanipal, the last strong Assyrian ruler, dies c. 626 B.C.

626 b.c. Nabopolassar becomes King of Babylon (626-605 B.C.) and begins to assert strength against Assyria. Egypt under Psammetichus (664-610 B.C.) likewise grows stronger. Young Jeremiah receives his call to be a prophet.

617-610 b.c. Under attack from Babylon and Media, Assyria crumbles. Nineveh falls in 612 B.C. Harran, to which the Assyrian leaders fled, falls in 610 B.C. despite help from Egypt. From 631 to 610, Judah under Josiah gains more and more independence, and Josiah is free to pursue his purge of pagan religious practices.

610 b.c. Neco succeeds Psammetichus in Egypt and determines to extend Egyptian influence.

609 b.c. Neco coming to the aid of the beleaguered Assyrians in Harran is met by Josiah at Megiddo. Josiah is slain and Judah's freedom comes to an abrupt end. Jehoahaz becomes king but Neco, threatened by the continuing feeling of Jewish nationalism, removes him, takes him to Egypt and sets up Jehoiakim as Egypt's vassal king. Jeremiah delivers the great Temple Sermon (26:1-22; 7:1—10:25).
609-605 b.c. Jehoiakim serves under Neco and builds for himself a larger palace. Jeremiah continues prophesying the destruction of Jerusalem and continues to find himself out of favor with king, princes, priests and people, as he counsels capitulation to Babylon.
605 b.c. Nebuchadnezzar II becomes King of Babylon (605-562 B.C.) and meets the Egyptians under Neco who have come to do battle at Carchemish. The Babylonians route the Egyptians and thus establish their power and make Jeremiah more convinced than ever that Judah has nothing to gain from her vassalage to Egypt.
604 b.c. Jehoiakim decides to submit to Nebuchadnezzar (Daniel and his friends are taken to Babylon at this time), but only for a time, for in 601 B.C. Jehoiakim is again courting Egypt's favor, despite Jeremiah's warnings.
598-597 b.c. In December the Babylonians attack Jerusalem and Jehoiakim dies. Jehoiachin is king for 3 months before Jerusalem capitulates in March 597 B.C. Nebuchadnezzar deports Jehoiachin and his court to Babylon (Ezekiel is also among the exiles) and sets up Zedekiah as his vassal king. The Babylonians also pillage the temple and carry off many of its treasures.
595 b.c. Psammetichus II becomes pharaoh in Egypt (595-589 B.C.).
594 b.c. In the ensuing years after the first "fall" of Jerusalem, Zedekiah continues to court Egypt's favor. In 594 B.C. Edom, Ammon and Moab (surrounding pagan "nations") consider with Judah how to throw off Babylon's yoke; this has the blessing of the "false" prophets and the condemnation of Jeremiah.

589 b.c. Hophra becomes pharaoh in Egypt (589-570 B.C.) and Zedekiah courts his favor. The Babylonians, taking this as rebellion, sweep down with their armies and capture Judah's fortified cities one by one. For a short time the siege of Jerusalem lifts as a task force from Egypt diverts the Babylonians' attention.

587 b.c. As a famine hits Jerusalem, the Babylonians capture the city and put an end to the kingdom of Judah. Most of the able-bodied are deported to Babylon and the city lies in ruins. Jeremiah, however, is treated with great respect and allowed to choose his future freely.

587-581 b.c. Gedeliah is appointed governor of Judah under Babylon with headquarters at Mizpah. Jeremiah stays with the remnant. By intrigue Gedeliah is slain and the remnant, again contrary to Jeremiah's advice, flees to Egypt. Jeremiah is taken along. In 581 B.C. a third deportation takes place and Judah, absorbed by Samaria, ceases any independent existence.

APPENDIX C

the kings of judah

Hezekiah	716-686 B.C. (co-regent with Ahaz from 729 B.C.)
Manasseh	686-641 B.C. (co-regent with Hezekiah from 696 B.C.)
Amon	641-639 B.C.
Josiah	639-609 B.C.
Jehoahaz	609 B.C. (3 months)
Jehoiakim	609-597 B.C.
Jehoiachin	597 B.C. (3 months)
Zedekiah	597-587 B.C.